Ancient Greek Jobs

Haydn Middleton

Heinemann Library
Chicago, Illinois

Text and cover designed by Tinstar
Originated by Ambassador Litho
Printed by Wing King Tong in Hong Kong.

07 06 05 04 03
10 9 8 7 6 5 4 3 2

Library of Congress Cataloging-in-Publication Data
Middleton, Haydn.
   Ancient Greek Jobs / Haydn Middleton.
      p. cm. -- (People in the past)
   Includes bibliographical references and index.
   Summary: Discusses ideas held about work in ancient Greece and
describes various occupations and what they entailed.
   ISBN 1-58810-638-1
   1. Work--Greece--History--Juvenile literature. 2.
Occupations--Greece--History--Juvenile literature. 3. Social
role--Greece--History--Juvenile literature. [1.
Work--Greece--History--To 146 B.C. 2. Occupations--Greece--History--To
146 B.C. 3. Greece--Social conditions--To 146 B.C.] I. Title. II.
Series.
   HD4902.5 .M53 2002
   331.7'00938--dc21

                            2001005215

Acknowledgments
The Publishers would like to thank the following for permission to reproduce photographs: Ancient Art and Architecture Collection, pp. 6, 16, 22, 25, 28, 30, 37, 38, 40; AKG London, pp. 7, 8, 13, 14, 17, 20, 23, 24, 32, 33, 34, 39; CM Dixon, p. 11; Richard Butler and Magnet Harlequin, pp. 12, 41; Michael Holford, pp. 19, 36; SCALA, p. 26.
Cover photograph reproduced with permission of AKG/Erich Lessing

Some words are shown in bold, **like this.** You can find out what they mean by looking in the glossary.

Contents

The World of the Ancient Greeks

When people talk about ancient Greece, they do not just mean the modern-day country of Greece as it used to be. The ancient Greek world was made up of the hot, rocky mainland of Greece and hundreds of islands in the Aegean, Ionian, and Adriatic Seas, as well as further settlements overseas, in places ranging from northern Africa to what we now call Turkey and Italy. The earliest Greek speakers did not think that they all belonged to a single country. For a long while, they did not even think that they all belonged to the same **civilization.**

From Minoans to Macedonians

For centuries, the mightiest people in the Greek world were the Minoans, based on the island of Crete. Power then passed to the warlike Mycenaeans, based on the mainland, in the region known as the **Peloponnese.** This was followed, around 1100 B.C.E., by centuries of confusion and upheaval, but since the art of writing was also lost, we know very little about this period. Later, in the Classical Age, from about 500 B.C.E. until about 300 B.C.E., prosperity was restored by the rise of many city-states, such as Athens. Most of the information in this book is about life in the city-states in this period. The Greek word for city-state is *polis.* Each *polis* controlled the villages and farmland around it. Each had its own laws and customs, and they often fought bitter wars against each other.

Daily life differed from one city-state to the next, but most of the men in them worked on the land as farmers. In the cities, other jobs needed to be done too—ranging from banking and sculpting to teaching and trading at the market. As you will discover, however, Greek people used to have different ideas about what kinds of work were honorable to do. Some **philosophers** even thought that **citizens,** who ran the *polis,* should not be distracted by work at all.

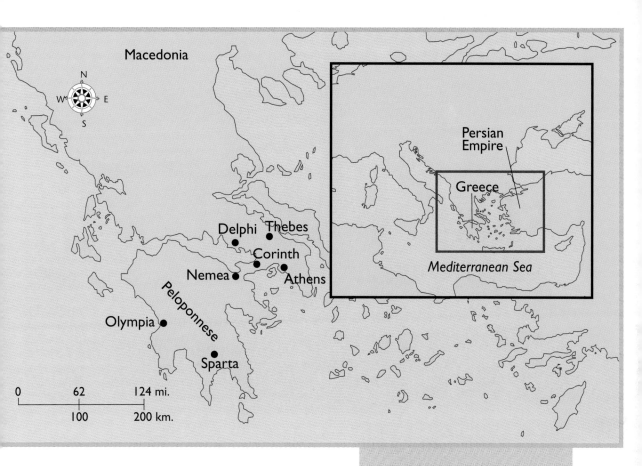

All Greeks were united by their common language and by their belief that their ways were superior to those of any foreign **barbarians.** Ancient Greek words, ideas, art forms, and attitudes still have a deep effect on us all today, more than 2,000 years since the Greek world was finally united under Alexander the Great, before it became a part of the Roman Empire.

Ancient Greece was not a single, unified country but was instead a collection of many separate states that often waged war on one another. The ancient Greeks used the word *Hellas* to mean all places where there was a Greek way of life.

Who Worked in Ancient Greece?

The picture above shows the Erechtheion, an ancient temple in Athens. Records survive from 405 B.C.E., telling us who built it. There were 71 workers under contract: 20 **citizens** of Athens; 35 *metics,* foreigners who lived in Athens; and 16 slaves. Of the managers on the job, three were citizens, two were *metics,* and one was a slave. All of them—free and unfree alike—were paid at the same rate. This was a ***drachma*** a day for a skilled worker, which was twice what an unskilled worker might earn.

Did many citizens work?

We do not always know exactly who worked on such big public projects or what they were all paid. It is harder still to discover details about the many lesser artisans and traders who worked in their own homes or in rough buildings attached to them. We can guess that most worked only during daylight hours, since there was no electric lighting, but not on festival days, which differed from place to place. We *do* know that some ancient Greek writers believed that freeborn citizens should not work at all.

This vase painting shows a shoemaker at work. He is pictured working alone, which might mean that he specialized in one area of shoemaking.

According to the writer Aristotle, citizens should not work "since leisure is necessary both for the development of virtue and [for] the performance of political duties." You can find out what some of these duties were on the next page.

In Classical Athens, many citizens did not actually need to work. Their incomes came from owning land, leasing city properties, or owning small "factories" and workshops. Some citizens, such as weavers and sculptors, did work, but they still enjoyed high **status.** However, no Athenian citizen would willingly work for long as a wage-earning employee for another citizen. By working for a master, he might seem to others to be little better than a slave. Although women did all kinds of domestic work, few did the sort of wage-earning work that men did. Their place was believed to be in the home. There was no such thing as equal opportunity in ancient Greece.

Early risers

In *The Birds*, a play by Aristophanes, one of the characters listed all the types of workers who had to make an early start: "When the cock sings his dawn song, up they all jump and rush off to work, the bronze-smiths, the potters, the tanners, the shoemakers, the bath-attendants, the corn-merchants, the **lyre**-shapers and shield-makers, and some of them even put on their sandals and leave when it's still dark." The Athenian historian Xenophon had no time for many of the craftsmen listed here, he wrote, "The bodies of those who do this work are damaged, since they are forced to sit down and work indoors. Some people even have to spend all day at the fire. As their bodies grow soft, so do their **characters.**"

The Citizen

"Man is above all a political animal," wrote Aristotle. The ancient Greeks took their politics very seriously, experimenting with all forms of government, from monarchy and **aristocracy** to **anarchy.** Many of the political terms that we use today—including "politics" itself—come from ancient Greek words. The **citizens** of each *polis* usually had at least some say in how they were governed. From about 500 B.C.E., citizens in Athens had more say than did those in most other places. That was when and where democracy was invented. Whereas, in modern **democracies,** millions of people vote in elections for others to govern them, in Classical Athens, the few thousand citizens governed themselves. For that reason, being a citizen was a vitally important job.

Direct democracy

The *ecclesia*, or citizens' assembly, met about 40 times a year on a hill outside Athens that was called the Pnyx. After some opening prayers, every citizen, rich or poor, was allowed to speak. Debates on big issues, such as whether Athens should go to war, could be turbulent. Meetings of the *ecclesia* were organized by the *boule*, a council of 500 elected members who all had to serve for one year. The *boule* met on every day that was not a festival day.

Pericles (around 495–429 B.C.E.) was a very important politician in Athens from 443 B.C.E. until his death. His brilliant speeches greatly influenced the citizens' decisions.

Among other duties, it supervised various boards of five or ten officials who kept the city running smoothly. There were boards to inspect weights and measures, to ensure that the roads were repaired, and to make sure that religious festivals were properly celebrated. In *The Constitution of Athens*, it was recorded that the board of the ten *astynomoi* had to check "that none of the dung-collectors dump dung within [two kilometers (about 1.25 miles)] of the city-wall. They also prevent the extending of houses into, and the building of balconies over, the streets … and they see to it that the girls who play the flute, the harp and the **lyre** are not hired for more than two **drachmas.**"

As well as serving as council members and public officials, citizens also had to take their turn each year as jurors, to give verdicts on quarrels between other citizens. They were given small fees to cover their expenses, but the rate of pay was poor: only half the amount paid to the skilled workers who built the Erechtheion at the **Acropolis** in Athens.

Roping in and voting out

Meetings of the *ecclesia* needed a **quorum** of 6,000 citizens. Sometimes, because these meetings were held early in the day or because some were too lazy to go to the Pnyx of their own accord, citizens had to be roped in—almost literally—from the **agora.** Scythian slaves went around touching idle citizens with a rope covered in red chalk or paint. Anyone so marked had to pay a fine. A more serious punishment was ostracism. Once a year, the citizens had a chance to banish anyone whom they disapproved. Votes were cast by scratching a name on a broken piece of pottery. If a total of 6,000 pieces was collected, the person with most votes against him had to leave the city for ten years.

The Slave

In 5th-century-B.C.E. Athens, there may have been 80,000–100,000 slaves. That was at least one slave for every free member of the population. Some experts believe there were many more. Most slaves were foreigners, such as **Persians** or Asians captured during warfare; some were the children of slaves. Slaves in Sparta, Thessaly, or Sicily often led hard lives, but in Athens it could be difficult to tell who was a slave and who was free.

A world without slaves

In his comedy *The Wild Animals*, the playwright Crates mocked the idea of **utopia,** where there were no male or female slaves. In that case, he said, all the household chores would have to do themselves. You can see what some were from his list: laying the table, kneading dough, pouring wine, washing cups, making bread, serving beef, and cooking fish.

"There is a very great lack of discipline among the slaves and *metics* in Athens," wrote historian Xenophon. "You are not allowed to strike a slave there, nor will a slave step aside for you.... Ordinary **citizens** there wear no better clothes than slaves or *metics*, and look no different." This may well have been true of domestic slaves. Some citizens bought slaves "to share their work with them," so they probably treated them decently, too. There were even some slaves who lived apart from their masters, paid them a proportion of their earnings, and saved up the rest to buy their freedom one day.

Human tools
The **philosopher** Aristotle called a slave "a living tool." Masters could treat their slaves as they chose, and only a foolish master would choose to mistreat his own tools. However, in the silver mines at Laurion in southeastern Attica, it was a different story. There, slaves probably outnumbered the free inhabitants.

Thousands of slaves worked underground, in appalling conditions. Kneeling or lying flat in tunnels just about 1.2 square yards (1 square meter), they had to dig out the ore by the light of small clay oil lamps. Other workers then dragged the silver ore away to the main shaft and carried it up a wooden staircase to the workshops, to be washed. Afterward it was **smelted** on the same site, giving rise to foul toxic fumes.

Many slaves from here must have been among the 20,000 who, according to Athenian historian Thucydides, escaped to Sparta toward the end of the **Peloponnesian** War (431–404 B.C.E.). In 135 B.C.E., there was a rare outbreak of mass violence involving more than 1,000 slaves. Their uprising was ruthlessly crushed before the trouble could spread.

This vase image from about 340 B.C.E. shows a domestic slave attending the mistress of her household. She might also be sent to market to shop for food.

The Priest and the Priestess

◄► ◄► ◄► ◄► ◄► ◄► ◄► ◄► ◄► ◄► ◄► ◄► ◄► ◄► ◄► ◄► ◄►

Ancient Greece was a land full of **deities.** Some were worshiped in the home, others in particular cities, and still others throughout the Greek-speaking world. Temples dotted the landscape, and the calendar was full of sacred festivals. Yet the priests who organized all this religious activity were not specially trained experts. They were just ordinary **citizens,** chosen to do the job part time. They were more like **civil servants** than professional religious leaders.

Getting the rituals right

In Athens, more than 40 priestesses were employed at major **shrines,** and some great festivals, such as the *Thesmophoria*, were celebrated only by women. Being a priestess was the only public job a woman was allowed. Male priests usually carried out sacrifices, while priestesses might weave clothes for temple statues. The main role that priests and priestesses played was carrying out all the necessary rituals, in the right order, at the right time, so that the deities would not turn against the city.

Particular gods or goddesses were worshiped in Greek temples. This one, built by Greeks in Italy, was dedicated to the sea god Poseidon, known later to the Romans as Neptune.

According to the writer Porphyry, this was how the *Dipolia* festival was celebrated: "They selected girls named water-carriers. They carried water so that the men could sharpen the axe and the knife. Of the men who did the sharpening one passed the axe, a second struck the ox, a third slit its throat. After this they skinned it and everyone had a share of the meat. When this was over they sewed up the ox hide, stuffed it with straw and stood it up, looking just as it did in life…. They then held a trial for murder [of the ox] and summoned all those who took part in the operation to make their defense. The water-carriers put the blame on those who did the sharpening. The sharpeners accused the man who handed over the axe, he blamed the man who struck the blow, he blamed the man who slit the throat, and he said the knife itself was guilty. Since the knife was incapable of speech, it was condemned for murder."

A sacrifice to the god Apollo is being made here. A priest would offer an animal's bones and inedible parts to the gods, while the edible meat was cooked and eaten.

Calling down curses

Priests and priestesses aimed to please their people's gods and goddesses and also tried to get these deities to punish the people's enemies. Around 470 B.C.E., the priests of the city of Teos, in Ionia, devised a curse to use on anyone who used poison against the Teians, prevented corn supplies from coming in, or betrayed the city in various other ways. The curse was then inscribed on stone and had to be uttered at three big festivals: the spring festival of *Anthesteria* and the festivals of Heracles and of Zeus.

The Teacher

There was not a great demand for teachers in ancient Greece. Only well-off **citizens** sent their sons to school, and usually they kept their daughters at home to learn the skills they would one day need as wives.

In different city-states there were different education systems. In Sparta, boys from the age of seven were brought up in **barracks,** not in family homes. The aim of Spartan teaching was to produce excellent warriors, and it was overseen by the *paidonomos,* a state director of education.

The government of Athens did not run special schools for citizens' sons. It probably did not even insist that they go to school. It just laid down laws that boys' journeys to and from the building take place in daylight and that the pupils aged seven to fourteen be protected from "bad influences."

This young man is writing on a wax plate with a device that is called a stylus.

Who were the teachers?

A *paidagogos*, or tutor, might accompany the boy at all times during the school day. He was a slave owned by the boy's father, and was responsible for his behavior, rather than his education. A *grammatistes* would teach the boy reading, writing, and simple arithmetic and would get him to learn by heart long passages from great poems such as Homer's *Iliad* and *Odyssey*. A *kitharistes*, or music teacher, would teach him the **lyre;** the *aulos*, which was like a double oboe; and singing. Then a *paidotribes* would supervise his physical education at the **palaestra.** This kind of education was popular in Athens before about 450 B.C.E., when teachers began to put more emphasis on style and grammar.

Teachers needed no special qualifications to do their job. Anyone could set himself up as a schoolmaster. Teachers' fees from parents seem to have been low, and so was their **status.** In the 4th century B.C.E., the great public speaker Demosthenes once taunted an opponent by saying, "Your childhood was spent in an atmosphere of great poverty. You had to help your father in his job as assistant teacher— preparing the ink, washing down the benches, sweeping out the classroom, and taking the rank of a slave rather than a freeborn boy."

Jokes about teachers

The abilities of ancient Greek teachers must have varied from school to school. Some did not have a high reputation among other citizens. Stories went around in which the *scholastikos*, or nutty professor, was ridiculed. In his book *Europe*, the modern historian Norman Davies records some of these stories. One tells about a *scholastikos* who wanted to see what he looked like when he was asleep, so he stood in front of a mirror with his eyes shut.

The Doctor

"We physicians base our diagnosis on our general knowledge of disease, and of particular diseases, and on our special knowledge of the illness we are treating, of the patient, his previous history and his previous doctor. Factors include the climate, the patient's origin, his way of life, his work, his age, his conversation, his **idiosyncracies,** his silences, his thoughts, his capacity for sleep, his dreams, their number and nature, any picking or scratching, **hysteria,** discharges, sneezing or sickness. We are **meticulous** in noting the progress of the illness to the critical point, checking such details as perspiration, chill, stiffness, coughs or sneezing, hiccupping, heavy breathing, internal bleeding. It is our professional duty to observe all these factors and their consequences."

So wrote Hippocrates, who ran a school of medicine on the island of Kos during the Classical Age. His approach sounds similar to that of modern doctors. In fact, many of his ideas had a lasting influence on medical theory and practice. Doctors today still take what's known as the Hippocratic oath.

Painful-looking instruments like these would have been used by ancient Greek doctors.

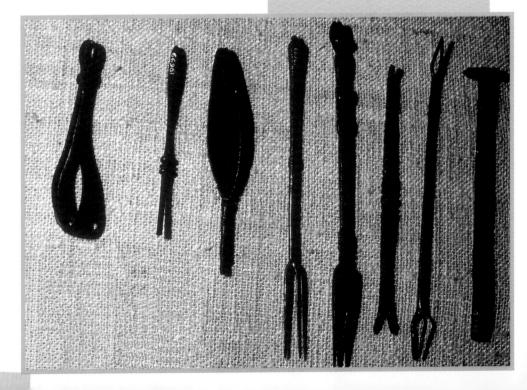

Before, during, and after Hippocrates' time, there were also a lot of nonscientific "healers" in ancient Greece. One writer called them "witch-doctors, faith-healers, quacks, and charlatans." They relied more on magic than on observation or experience. Yet even proper doctors, who might train for many years under their fathers or masters, took no degrees or other qualifications, so they were judged by the results of their treatments. Since their patients had to pay them for their visits, their **livelihoods** depended on that, too.

Celebrity doctors

The effect that most doctors had was limited, for the Greeks had little grasp of the causes of disease, and a **taboo** stopped them from dissecting the human body to find out more about its workings. Some doctors, such as Demokedes from Kroton, made great names for themselves—and became very wealthy. The historian Herodotus recorded that the island of Aegina paid him one *talent* a year as resident physician. That was twenty times as much as an average skilled worker made. Then, at Samos, he was employed at a rate of two *talents* a year.

The medical expert Hippocrates (c. 460–377 B.C.E.) is called "the father of medicine" because of his sensible and kind treatment of his patients.

The Merchant

From very early times, the Greeks were a busy trading people. Island traded with island, and city traded with city—and Athens was the biggest city of them all. Most trade was carried out by sea, since overland travel was costly and difficult in a land with few good roads. The map below shows how far afield merchants traveled, often to Greek **colonies** in North Africa and Western Europe, and the goods they brought back. In small, slow, rounded wooden vessels with a single mast and a large, square-rigged sail, they braved the seas without charts, compasses, or other vital navigational aids.

Risk-taking traders

A merchant was often the owner of a single ship, of which he was the master. If he had no ship, he might hire cargo space from a shipowner. He might also have to take out a loan, to pay for all or some of the cargo. In that case, he could turn to a banker or moneylender to help him out.

Many merchants were seen as rough and ready, only interested in profit. Often they were foreigners, called *metics,* so they did not enjoy high **status.** It is unlikely that they cared much about that. They had enough on their minds already. With every voyage, their goods could be lost in shipwrecks, be stolen by pirates, or simply turn out to be unfit for sale at market.

N W E S

SCYTHIA
timber, slaves

Olbia

Dioscurias

Massalia

ITALY
meat, copper,
wool, linen

THRACE
iron, copper,
grain, slaves

Odessus

Sinope
iron, fish,
nuts

Neapolis
MACEDONIA
timber, gold,
silver

Heraclea

Sybaris
Croton

Phoecaea

ASIA MINOR

Selinus
Sicily
grain,
timber

Syracuse

Corinth
Sparta

Athens
oil, wine,
silver, pottery,
metalwork

Miletus

Al Mina

CARTHAGE
rugs, cushions

Rhodes

Phaselis

Crete

Cyprus
grain, oil,
timber,
copper

Salamis

SYRIA
slaves,
dates,
dyes

Cyrene
wool, grain,
silphium,
vegetables

Naucratis

EGYPT
grain, papyrus,
flax, ivory

● Greek homeland cities
● Greek colonies

These were the main Greek colonies in the Mediterranean and Black Seas. You can see what goods they produced and traded among colonies.

Historians once thought that traders always hugged the coasts on their voyages and sailed, if possible, only during the day. In 2001, archaeologists discovered a sunken Greek trading ship between Rhodes and Alexandria, right in the middle of the Mediterranean Sea. Four similar wrecks are believed to lie nearby. More discoveries like this may one day find that really daring Greek traders often made long-distance voyages across open seas too.

This vase is decorated with a painting of a merchant ship powered by sail. It was made around 540 B.C.E.

Supply and demand

Merchants had to be good businessmen. This often involved buying goods cheaply and selling them at high prices. The Athenian historian Xenophon wrote of traders who "from their passion for grain, sail in search of it wherever they hear it is most abundant, crossing over the Aegean, Euxine, and Sicilian Seas. And when they have got as much of it as they can, they bring it away over the water, stowing it in the vessel in which they themselves sail. And when they are in want of money, they carry their freight to … wherever they hear that grain will fetch the highest price, and offer it for sale."

The Banker

"The resources required by those who engage in trade come not from those who borrow, but from those who lend; and neither ship nor ship-owner nor passenger can put to sea, if you take away the part contributed by those who lend." Not surprisingly, the speaker here, a man named Chrysippus, was himself a moneylender, or banker. He was complaining to a jury in Classical Athens that he had been cheated by a *metic* merchant to whom he had lent 2,000 **drachmas,** to finance a trading voyage to the Bosphorus Sea.

Bankers were indeed very important when traders needed large sums of money. They made the most of this by charging high rates of interest for each voyage.

These coins, found with this **terra-cotta** jug, date back to the 4th century B.C.E. After coins were introduced into Greece from Lydia, in about 600 B.C.E., coin hoards like this one were often buried to keep them safe.

Successful slaves

We know of about twenty bankers in Classical Athens. The most successful was a man named Pasion. Remarkably, he began his working life as another banker's slave. Around 400 B.C.E., he gained his freedom, took over his master's business, and even became a **citizen** by a decree of the people, despite his low birth. When he died, it was said that he was worth almost 60 *talents.* (In 431 B.C.E., there were only 6,000 *talents* in the entire Athenian treasury.) Then his own slave, Phormio, rose to be made a citizen, too.

Almost all bankers were *metics*, and many were ex-slaves. Very few followed in the rags-to-riches footsteps of Pasion and Phormio. Their services were used mainly by other *metics*. This was because many citizens preferred to rely on friends, neighbors, or relatives when they needed to make a deposit or take out a loan. However, citizens might use bankers as money changers, since so many different coins were used in the ancient Greek world.

Banking practices

"When a private individual deposits money with the instruction that it is to be paid to a particular person, the banker begins by writing the depositor's name and the sum of money, and then he writes alongside 'to be paid to X.' If the banker knows by sight the person to whom the payment is to be made, then he just has to write his name. If he does not, he adds the name of a person who will identify and introduce to him the person who is to receive the money."

Athenian politician Demosthenes recorded this system of exchange. Compared to modern banking, with personal checks and credit cards, Greek banking does not seem very secure.

The Farmer

Most Greeks worked on the land, but Greece is not a very fertile country. Only about one-fifth of it is cultivated today; in ancient times it was probably the same. Lowland farmers mainly grew grains such as barley and wheat and grapes for wine and, most important, olives. Olive oil was used for cooking, for lamp-fuel, and also as a substitute for soap. Farmers grew so many olives that they had enough for their own needs and then sold the rest for some extra cash. Farmers on higher ground kept bees for honey, small numbers of sheep and pigs, and also goats for milk and cheese. To grow any crops, they first had to cut terraces into the rocky mountain slopes, which was always a tough job.

Farming communities

A few farmers were extraordinarily rich men, who spent most of their time in the city and let **overseers** run their farms. In Classical times, a landowner named Phaenippus had an annual income of about 30,000 **drachmas,** while skilled workers earned only one *drachma* a day. Most farmers, however, owned or rented very small farms—maybe only four or five acres in size—and lived together in villages to protect and support one another.

This view of the modern Greek countryside around Athens, shows one of many regions that must have been hard to farm during ancient times.

Farmers often struggled to make a living. Poor rainfall in Attica, the region around Athens, meant that they might lose their entire wheat crop once every four years. Their aim was to produce enough food for themselves and their families and a little more to sell in the nearest city.

City dwellers depended heavily on what farmers grew but did not always treat them with a great deal of respect. The teacher and writer Theophrastus made fun of a **rustic** in the late 4th century B.C.E. This country person seems enthusiastic, and almost childlike: "If he has lent someone a plow, basket, sickle or bag, he goes to ask for it back in the middle of the night … and when he is going to the city, he asks anyone he meets about the price of hides and salt fish … and he says right away that, when he gets there, he's going to have his hair cut, have his shoes re-soled … and have a good sing in the public baths."

Farming against the odds

In Greece, the climate is hot and dry, the landscape is mountainous, and much of the soil is thin and hard to farm. As early as the 6th century B.C.E., Greek rulers tried to make sure that the land was looked after. Farmers were given a reward for planting new olive trees, to keep up their numbers. The **philosopher** Plato wrote, however, that "what now remains … is like the skeleton of a sick man, all the fat and soft earth having wasted away. There are some mountains which now have nothing but food for bees, but they had trees a year ago, and boundless pastures."

This vase shows farm workers picking olives. Olive trees grew well in the poor Greek soil. The trees also provided welcome shade from the hot sun.

The Fisher and the Fish Seller

◀▷ ◀▷ ◀▷ ◀▷ ◀▷ ◀▷ ◀▷ ◀▷ ◀▷ ◀▷ ◀▷ ◀▷ ◀▷ ◀▷ ◀▷ ◀▷ ◀▷

One of the great mariners of Greek myth was Odysseus. For ten years after the siege of Troy, he and his men sailed the seas before returning home to Ithaca. His thrilling story is told in Homer's epic poem, *The Odyssey*. Scholars have noted that, on all their travels, these famous sailors hardly ever seemed to eat fish. When they put ashore, their banquets featured roasted meats instead.

Once, when the sailors landed on the island of the sun god's cattle, "all the food in the ship was gone and they were forced instead to go roaming in search of prey, using bent hooks to catch fish and birds, anything that might come to hand, because hunger gnawed their bellies." It seems that they looked on fish as poor men's food, not suitable for heroes. This is odd, because by Classical times fish became the most desirable of all foods, which was fortunate, since there were so many fish in the seas off the Greek coastline.

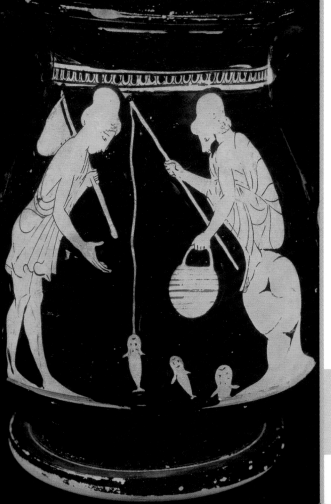

Writing about fish

Writers continued to say little about the men who caught these fish. They sold catches of little fish such as anchovies and sprats to the poor and supplied such delicacies as electric rays, tuna, sea bass, red mullet, and crayfish to the better off. There were no refrigerators, so fish had to be sold quickly or preserved in salt, although salt fish was looked down on as a cheap substitute.

Fish-catching techniques seem to have changed remarkably little since ancient Greek times.

Many fish were baked and served whole. This decorated Greek plate has a small recess or dent at its center. It was used for storing the sauce that went with the fish.

Although Greek writers largely ignored fishers, they had plenty to say about fish sellers, especially dishonest ones. In a collection of stories, the ancient Greek writer Apuleius told about how a man haggled with a fish seller for a basket of fish. He got the price down from 200 to 20 **drachmas** and paid for the fish, but as he took the basket away, the market inspector intervened. The inspector was so upset by the poor quality of the fish that he emptied the basket on the ground. Then he ordered his officer to jump on the fish until they were mashed into paste. He apologized to the customer, but explained that his actions were necessary to punish the fish seller for selling bad fish. The customer departed, amazed that he had lost both his money and his dinner.

Favorite fish

Most ancient writers agree that the most highly valued item on any fish seller's stall was the eel. It was believed that fishers who worked on the waters between Sicily and the "toe" of boot-shaped Italy caught the choicest eels. "All in all I think the eel rules over everything else at the feast," was the view of the writer Archestratus, "despite being the only fish with no backbone."

The Market Trader

Pausanias defined a city-state as a place that had government offices, a gymnasium, a theater, an **agora,** and a fountain. An *agora* was vital to the life of any Greek city. The word *agora* is usually translated as "marketplace." According to the historian Herodotus, the King of Persia called it "a special place marked out where Greeks meet to cheat each other."

This vase painting shows a fishmonger chopping up fish for a customer. Fresh fish would have been available to buy daily at the *agora*.

The hub of the city

Artisans could sell their wares at the *agora,* as well as from their workshops. It was also a place for having meetings, hiring workers, watching entertainment, and putting criminals on trial. "In one and the same place," wrote the comic poet Eubulus, "you will find all kinds of things for sale together at Athens: figs, **bailiffs,** bunches of grapes, turnips, pears, apples, witnesses, roses, **medlars,** puddings, honeycombs, chickpeas, lawsuits, ... curds, myrtle, ... irises, lambs, water-clocks, laws and **indictments.**"

Different types of goods and services were sold in different parts of the market: olive oil was sold on the east side, and barbers set up shop on the north side, along with bankers, who sat at counters to make loans or change money. The goods were laid out on flimsy stalls, although some traders had small covered shops, the walls and roofs of which were made of reeds. It must have been hot, dusty, and very noisy.

Wealthy women did not visit the *agora* unless they were looking for perfume or fashionable jewelry. Their husbands or slaves did the daily shopping and then had it sent back to the house with a slave or servant. There were no shopping bags. Aristophanes described soldiers buying vegetable **puree** and taking it away in their helmets. Male Athenian shoppers seem to have carried small change in their mouths.

From 374 B.C.E., public testers of silver coins sat every day at a certain spot in the *agora* with weighing scales. They weighed the coins to make sure that they contained enough silver to be worth the right amount. These testers were usually slaves. If he failed to appear for work, the tester was beaten as a reminder to do his duty.

Fair trade?

Customers haggled, or bargained, with traders over the prices of their goods. Just as in some markets today, there were inevitably some dishonest traders around. Greek writers complained about overcharging, as well as the traders' bad backgrounds. Market inspectors tried to ensure fair trade.

The Craftsman

The Athenian historian Xenophon wrote, "In small towns the same person makes doors, beds, plows, tables; he's often a builder too; and even so he is delighted if he finds enough work to keep him going. And, of course, a jack-of-all-trades is master of none. In large cities there are plenty of customers for any one branch of industry, and one branch of industry or even a **subdivision** of it is enough to support an individual. So one worker specializes in male footwear, another in female. In some places one man earns his living by stitching shoes, another by cutting them out, another by simply sewing the **uppers** together, without any specialized skill except rounding the job off. So anyone who is proposing to concentrate on a highly specialized job is bound to be supremely good at it."

This painting shows two blacksmiths working at a furnace. Blacksmiths had to heat charcoal, their usual fuel, to temperatures high enough to properly reduce the ore. Otherwise the resulting metal would be impure, causing it to break easily.

Small-scale industry

In big cities, craftsmen of the same kind had their workshops in a single area. In Athens, the potters' quarter was called the *Kerameikos*. By working so closely together, craftsmen could exchange ideas and compete to produce the finest products.

Craftsmen's workshops, even in cities, were quite small. A **metic** named Kephalos owned an armor-making "factory" in Athens, and he employed 120 slaves. That was unusual. The father of the Athenian politician Demosthenes ran a workshop with twenty carpenters who made beds; a man named Timarchos ran a business staffed by nine shoemakers and one manager. Sometimes craftsmen just worked in their own homes or in buildings added on to them. They might be free citizens, slaves, or *metics*; sometimes all three kinds of people worked under the same roof. The average pay seems to have been a **drachma** a day for a skilled worker, which was also what soldiers or sailors on campaign were paid.

The Potter

In the Classical Age (about 500–300 B.C.E.), the Greeks did not set artists apart from other workers. Along with blacksmiths, carpenters, and shoemakers, they were all involved in *techne,* or craft, from which we get our word "technology." Some of their handiwork could be so fine that it has survived as the highest art.

Most crafts were practiced among families. Boys would naturally become apprentices to their fathers, whose workers and slaves they would assist and whose skills they would learn. Usually there were no more than ten men in a workshop. Each town or village would have its own pottery, using local supplies of clay. Potters mainly served local needs and often produced vases in styles particular to their area.

From the 6th century B.C.E., however, for about 150 years, Athenian pottery became popular across a very wide area. Pottery does not decay, so it has since been found all over the Mediterranean region.

Black figures, red figures

Athenian clay, rich in iron, turned a reddish color when it was fired in a kiln. Before firing, artists used to decorate their pots with a mixture of clay, water, and wood ash, scratching on any details with a pointed tool. After firing, the decorations turned out black, and the backgrounds turned out red. After about 510 B.C.E., a red-figure style became more popular.
The backgrounds were black, and the figures were red, but with details outlined in black with a fine brush, which gave more fluid lines than a scratching tool.

Practical and beautiful

Pottery objects had all sorts of uses in the home and in religious rituals. Vases were vital containers for liquids such as olive oil or for solids such as grain, since the Greeks lacked modern materials such as plastics and cardboard. Potters made vases of all shapes and sizes, including *amphorae,* to use for the storage of wine, and *kraters,* to use as cups for wine and water. Those that were painted give us information on all aspects of Greek life.

As in sculpture, Greek vase painting grew more and more realistic over time. Painters paid special attention to the human figure and tried to see how people's inner feelings affected the body in action. They tried, according to the **philosopher** Socrates, "to represent the workings of the human soul." In the 5th century B.C.E., some of them produced work that matched this ideal.

This extremely old vase dates back to the 8th century B.C.E. Its decorations, which include images of warriors and of a boat, provide useful information for historians.

The Sculptor

"To Phyromachus of Cephisia, for the figure of the young man by the breastplate: 60 **drachmas.**

"To Praxias, resident of Melite, for the figures of the horse and the man behind turning it: 120 *drachmas*.

"To Antiphanes of Cerameis, for the figures of the chariot, young man and pair of horses being yoked: 240 *drachmas*."

These are part of the **accounts** for a public building project in Athens in 407 B.C.E. The men being paid were sculptors. They seem to have been paid at a rate of 60 *drachmas* for each figure that they produced, but we cannot say how long each figure took to make. Some of the men in these accounts were not natives of Athens. Good sculptors tended to move around as they practiced their trade.

We know the names of some of the most famous Greek sculptors: Polykleitos, in the 5th century B.C.E.; and Praxiteles, Skopas, and Lysippos, in the 4th century B.C.E. However, almost none of their masterpieces have survived because sculptors most often worked in either stone, which breaks quite easily, or in bronze, which was usually melted down and reused for other purposes. Fortunately, Roman copies of some great sculptures do still exist.

The elusive Phidias

The biggest, greatest surviving sculptures are the marble decorations of the Parthenon. Its **frieze** was a continuous band 525 feet (160 meters) long, and there were also two beautifully decorated **pediments.** All this work was done in less than ten years, around 440 to 432 B.C.E., so several master sculptors must have been involved. Their **overseer** was named Phidias.

A statue of a boxer from the 1st century B.C.E. is shown here. The signature of the sculptor—Appollonis, son of Nestor—appears on the leather bindings around the boxer's hands.

This magnificent statue dates back to the 1st century B.C.E. Made from a single block of marble, it shows the mythical figure Laocoon and his sons being squeezed to death by serpents. In was discovered in a Roman vineyard in 1506.

Large-scale projects such as the building of the Parthenon were, however, hard to carry through in times of war, when public funds were being used for military purposes.

Greek writers described Phidias's other works of genius, which have since disintegrated or been destroyed. Among them were a huge gold and ivory figure of Zeus at Olympia and a vast bronze statue of Athena that stood, facing Propylaea, on the **Acropolis.** We know disappointingly little about Phidias or his methods of work, but his style influenced Athenian sculpture until at least the end of the 5th century B.C.E.

Domestic sculpture

Archaeologists often find small sculptures in people's graves. They show that sculptors did not just make huge statues, paid for by the city-state's government, to stand in public places. Sculpted household figures or objects could be ingeniously artistic—for example, pairs of **terra-cotta** feet that are actually little bottles of perfume. Sculptors brought to their workshops a wide variety of materials, ranging from marble, limestone, and sandstone to gold, silver, lead, bronze, and iron. They even worked in ivory, bone, and **amber** and made statuettes from painted wood and beeswax to be displayed in people's homes.

The Athlete

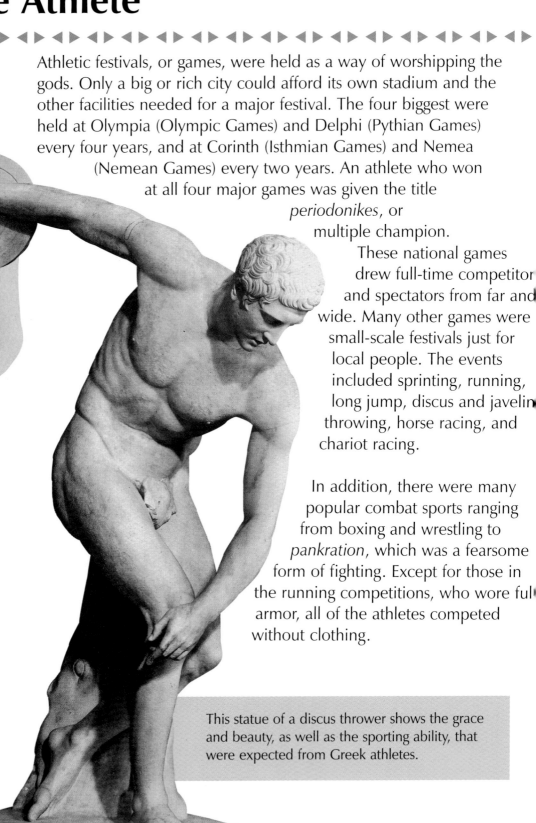

Athletic festivals, or games, were held as a way of worshipping the gods. Only a big or rich city could afford its own stadium and the other facilities needed for a major festival. The four biggest were held at Olympia (Olympic Games) and Delphi (Pythian Games) every four years, and at Corinth (Isthmian Games) and Nemea (Nemean Games) every two years. An athlete who won at all four major games was given the title *periodonikes*, or multiple champion.

These national games drew full-time competitor and spectators from far and wide. Many other games were small-scale festivals just for local people. The events included sprinting, running, long jump, discus and javelin throwing, horse racing, and chariot racing.

In addition, there were many popular combat sports ranging from boxing and wrestling to *pankration*, which was a fearsome form of fighting. Except for those in the running competitions, who wore full armor, all of the athletes competed without clothing.

This statue of a discus thrower shows the grace and beauty, as well as the sporting ability, that were expected from Greek athletes.

Classical superstars

Ancient Olympic champions won great fame. They were like modern sports heroes and movie stars rolled into one. Theogenes of Thasos, who won competitions at more than 1,200 festivals, including three Olympic crowns, was worshiped as a god after his death. A legend says that when an old opponent defaced a statue honoring Theogenes, in Thasos, it toppled over and crushed him to death. The best athletes traveled from festival to festival, competing for glory and winning wreaths of olive or laurel leaves. These were like the gold, silver, and bronze medals that athletes compete for today. However, the ancient Greek athletes were not pure **amateurs.** When they went home to their own city-states, they often received gifts of money or food from their fans and admirers. Therefore, unlike most people, they were able to eat plenty of meat, to put on extra weight and muscle. Trainers and coaches paid very close attention to athletes' diets as they prepared for big games.

Athletes were always expected to compete honorably. At the big games, competitors and officials alike took an oath to stick to the rules and neither offer nor take bribes. Cheating was punished by attendants with whips, who were kept on standby. No one was supposed to forget that the prime purpose of athletics was not to win at all costs, but to show devotion to the gods.

Ultimate combat

Pankration, meaning complete strength or complete victory, was an ancient Olympic combat sport. Strangleholds, attacking the eyes, kicking, breaking fingers, and dislocating limbs were all used in an attempt to put down an opponent. Top *pankratiasts* were big men. The first Olympic victor, Lygdamis of Syracuse, was said to be a giant whose feet were about 18 inches (45 centimeters) long. These champions also had to be determined. There was no time limit, except nightfall, for the exhausting fights, so *kartereia*, meaning endurance, was a good quality to have.

The Actor

As with the athlete, the Greek actor did his work as a way of worshipping the gods. Plays developed from religious choral dances, in honor of the **deity** Dionysus. First, one actor, usually the poet who had written the words, began to speak in **dialogue** with the rest of the chorus. This was made up of twelve to fifteen actors. In later years, a second, then a third actor, would come forward, while the chorus danced, sang, and commented on the action. There were never more than three solo actors, and they were always men, since women were not allowed to perform in the theater. In the Classical Age (about 500–300 B.C.E.), professional groups of actors toured Greece, performing wherever they were required.

Competitive drama

In Classical Athens, one of the year's greatest events was the springtime *Dionysia* festival. Its main feature was a drama competition, lasting for four days in an open-air theater that still lies on the southern slope of the **Acropolis.** Since it was a religious festival, the city government went to a lot of trouble organizing it and paying for it. The chief **magistrate** for the year chose which poets' plays should be performed, and he made sure that wealthy **citizens** paid for the training and costumes of the chorus.

On this vase from the 4th century B.C.E., actors perform a comedy. They are wearing the masks and padded clothing that were typical of theater.

These are modern versions of the kind of masks worn by actors in ancient Greece. Big masks were used to show everyone in a large audience clearly whether a character was happy or sad.

When all the plays, usually four per day, had been performed, a panel of citizen judges voted on which play was the best. Then prizes were awarded not only to the poet and the actors, but also to the citizen who had financed the show. The festivals were hugely popular. About 14,000 spectators crammed inside the theater. They came from all walks of life, paying two **obols** to get in if they could afford it, or nothing if they were poor. Women were not supposed to be admitted, but it seems that sometimes they were. Actors were pelted with stones or food from the audience's packed lunches if they did not put on a good enough show.

First and best

The Greeks devised the first plays in the world, and since some are still performed today, these plays must rank among the best ever written. Actors put on their masks to appear in tragedies or comedies. Tragic actors wore richly colored, flowing robes and special boots called *kothornoi*. Comic actors wore lots of padding and flat slippers to make them look ridiculous. Unfortunately, of all the dramas written by playwrights such as Aeschylus, Sophocles, Euripides, and Aristophanes, only a fraction survive—but they do give us a wealth of information on life and attitudes in ancient Greece.

The Thinker

"A life without asking questions," said Socrates, "is no life at all." What he meant was *big* questions—about the lives of individuals and the ways of the universe. Most Greek people were too busy in their daily jobs to spend much time pondering ideas. However, a number of men were paid to devote their lives just to philosophy—that is, thinking, investigating, discussing, and exchanging ideas, as well as maybe even setting up schools to teach others to think for themselves too. Some of these **philosophers** were the greatest thinkers the world has ever known. Their ideas continue to influence the way in which we look at the world in the 21st century.

World-class wise men

Before the Classical Age, two notable thinkers were Heraclitus of Ephesus and Pythagoras, who set up a school at Kroton. Heraclitus believed that everything in the world is always changing. "You cannot step into the same river twice," he liked to say. Pythagoras was a brilliant mathematician, and we still use his ideas today. He was also a **mystic** who taught his students that the souls of the dead moved on into other bodies.

Sometimes Classical philosophers got into trouble by challenging existing ideas, especially religious ones. Socrates, the son of a stonemason, was told by the **oracle at Delphi** that he was the wisest man in Greece. This baffled him, since he thought that he knew very little. He decided that he must be wise because he *knew* that he knew so little. He sought to learn more by asking questions, but the Athenians decided that he was corrupting the minds of his young students and sentenced him to death by drinking **hemlock.**

For a while, Aristotle, shown in this mosaic, was a tutor to the future Alexander the Great of Macedonia.

Schools of thought

Some thinkers attracted groups, or schools, of followers. The followers of Pyrrhon of Elis were called the Skeptics. They believed that people could be certain of nothing, so they should just try to be good. The Cynics who followed Diogenes of Sinope, an eccentric who lived in a barrel to show his hatred of worldly comforts and possessions, thought that people should free themselves from all desire. Epicurus of Samos taught his Epicureans to seek happiness through self-control, while Cyprus's Stoics—named after the *Stoa poikile*, or painted porch, in Athens, where they first met—believed in accepting their fate, whatever it was, but trying to lead good and honorable lives anyway. *Cynic, skeptic, epicurean*, and *stoic* are all words used in English today.

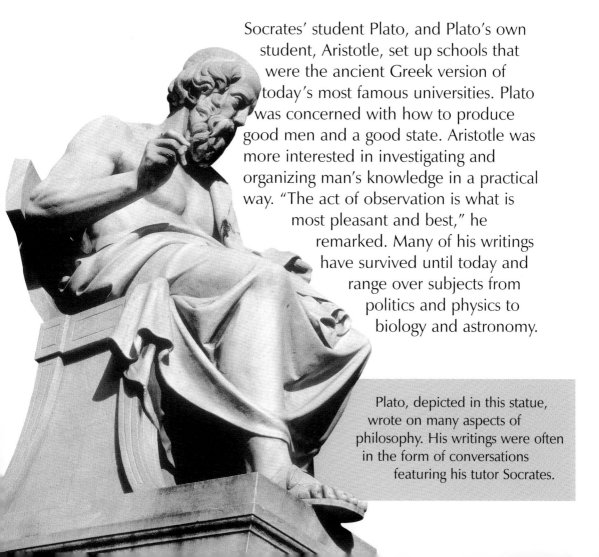

Socrates' student Plato, and Plato's own student, Aristotle, set up schools that were the ancient Greek version of today's most famous universities. Plato was concerned with how to produce good men and a good state. Aristotle was more interested in investigating and organizing man's knowledge in a practical way. "The act of observation is what is most pleasant and best," he remarked. Many of his writings have survived until today and range over subjects from politics and physics to biology and astronomy.

Plato, depicted in this statue, wrote on many aspects of philosophy. His writings were often in the form of conversations featuring his tutor Socrates.

The Architect

The picture below shows the magnificent outdoor theater at Epidauros. It is still used every summer, for modern audiences to sit on the same seats and see the same plays as ancient Greek people did, well over 2,000 years ago. It was designed by the architect Polyclitus and was built into the hillside in about 350 B.C.E. According to the much traveled writer Pausanias, it was the finest theater in ancient Greece.

The Greeks liked to be surrounded by beauty, so they took a lot of notice of their public buildings—and of the men who designed them. In Classical times, the governments of city-states like Athens were prepared to pay for the best architects to give them the temples, theaters, and treasuries they wanted.

The Athenians, for example, employed an architect for a new temple of Athena Nike on the **Acropolis.** An **inscription** from the first half of the 5th century B.C.E. recorded the appointment: "Resolved by the council and assembly … a temple and a stone altar will be built according to specifications drawn up by Callicrates.… Three men will be chosen from the council to assist him, and will indicate how the building work is to be **contracted** out." In some people's opinion, work like Callicrates' has not been improved on ever since.

The site of this ancient stone theater is Epidauros, in the **Peloponnese.** Earlier Greek stage buildings and seating areas were made of wood.

The quest for proportion

No books specializing in architecture survive from ancient Greece. The Roman architect Vitruvius did, however, pay homage to the Greek masters. "The planning of temples," he wrote, "depends upon symmetry.… It arises from proportion [which, in Greek, is called *analogia*].… Without symmetry and proportion no temple can have a regular plan; that is, it must have an exact proportion worked out after the fashion of the members of a finely-shaped human body."

Architects worked miracles with great blocks of marble or limestone, cut from Greece's plentiful quarries. They directed workers to join

these together with metal clamps and pins set in lead, not with **mortar**—making the joints almost invisible. They also used ingenious optical illusions to ensure that high buildings still seemed to be in proportion when viewed from below.

At the Erechtheion temple in Athens, six statues of women took the place of columns, to hold up the tops of the pillars.

How Do We Know? The Acropolis

We know from Classical writings that a big *polis* would have an acropolis, a fortress in a high place, where the **citizens** could take refuge in times of danger. In 490 B.C.E., or just before, the **Acropolis** in Athens was destroyed by the invading **Persians.** When the Athenians reclaimed their city, the citizens' assembly decided to pay for a new Acropolis and included a temple that was even more splendid than before. This temple was the Parthenon, which was built between about 447 and 432 B.C.E.

"Eagle among the clouds"

Restored and repaired, the Parthenon still stands and, as well as astounding us with its beauty, it tells us a lot about the past. We can see the limestone foundations, the marble blocks so precisely shaped by stonemasons, and the statues sculpted under the supervision of the artist Phidias. We can even read the annual building **accounts** for the whole project, which are inscribed on a pillar in the Acropolis. Those for 434–433 B.C.E. show that a balance of 1,470 *drachmas* was carried over from the previous year, with 25,000 *drachmas* coming in from the treasurers of the temple of Athena and with various wages paid to workers "for quarrying on Mount Pentelicus and loading stone into carts."

The Parthenon looks like this today. The height of each column is four-ninths the width of the building. The width of each column is four-ninths the distance between them.

These are the roof tiles, which covered the wooden frame of the Parthenon roof.

Buildings are made to last. So we know more about the work of ancient Greek builders and architects than we do about that of fishsellers, athletes, actors, and certain other workers. From the writings of Plutarch, we even know the names of the architects who worked on the Parthenon: Callicrates and Ictinus. Today, the Acropolis survives to be marveled at. It is amazing to think that when the Parthenon first took shape high above Athens, on the streets below walked Greeks of such genius as Socrates, Hippocrates, and Thucydides—alongside great numbers of the vital workers you have read about in this book. Athens was fulfilling the prophecy of the **oracle at Delphi:** "You will become an eagle among the clouds for all time."

An enduring achievement

The builders of the Parthenon would have been amazed at what happened to their great work. It later became a Christian church and afterward, when the Muslim Turks made Greece a part of their empire, it was a mosque. The Turks then used it to store gunpowder, and in 1687 C.E., an army from Venice blew it up during a war. Later, Lord Elgin, a British ambassador to Turkey, had many of the marble carvings brought to London, where they are still displayed in the British Museum.

Timeline

All the following dates are B.C.E.:

c. 3000–c. 1450   Greece is controlled by Minoan kings, from Crete.

c. 1600–c. 1100   Greek-speaking Mycenaeans rule separate kingdoms in mainland Greece.

c. 1100–c. 800   Greece goes through a period of wars and migration.

c. 800–c. 700   Homer's *Iliad* and *Odyssey* were probably written Greece is made up of small city-states that are ruled by separate kings or noble families.

c. 750–c. 550   Greeks set up colonies in lands around the Mediterranean Sea.

c. 500   Some city-states become democracies; of these, Athens is the most powerful.

c. 490–479   The main period of **Persian** invasions of Greece occurs.

431–404   The **Peloponnesian** War, between Greek city-states, ends with Sparta eclipsing Athens as the most powerful state in mainland Greece.

378–371   Sparta is eclipsed by a new power, Thebes.

336–323   Greece is ruled by Alexander the Great of Macedon after his invasion and conquest.

146   Greece becomes part of the Roman Empire.

More Books to Read

Barron's Educational Editors. *Greek Life*. Hauppage, N.Y.: Barron's
    Educational Services, Inc., 1998.

Bartole, Mira, and Christine Ronan. *Ancient Greece*. Parsippany,
    N.J.: Pearson Learning, 1995.

Clare, John D., ed., *Ancient Greece*. New York: Harcourt
    Children's Books, 1994.

Day, Nancy. *Your Travel Guide to Ancient Greece*. Minneapolis: Lerner
    Publishing Group, 2000. An older reader can help you with this
    book.

Ganeri, Anita. *Ancient Greeks*. Danbury, Conn.: Franklin Watts, 1993.

Greene, Jacqueline. *Slavery in Ancient Greece and Rome*. Danbury, Conn.:
    Franklin Watts, 2001. An older reader can help you with this book.

MacDonald, Fiona, and Mark Bergin. *A Greek Temple*. Columbus, Ohio:
    McGraw-Hill Children's Publishing, 1992.

Malam, John. *A Greek Town*. Danbury, Conn.: Franklin Watts, 1999.

Nardo, Don. *Life in Ancient Greece*. Farmington Hills, Mich.: The Gale Group,
    1996. An older reader can help you with this book.

Pearson, Anne. *Ancient Greece*. New York: Dorling-Kindersley
    Publishers, Inc., 2000.

Rees, Rosemary. *The Ancient Greeks*. Chicago: Heinemann Library, 1997.

Glossary

account financial record

Acropolis high-up fortress in Athens, where the citizens could take refuge in times of danger

agora marketplace

amateur player who competes merely for the love of the game, not for money

amber yellow fossilized material

anarchy lack of any kind of government

aristocracy rule by the best citizens in a state, often determined by wealth

bailiff official, often in a court of law

barbarian anyone who was not Greek

barracks building or buildings in which soldiers live apart from other people

character personality

citizen person with the right to take part in politics, in particular, by voting

civilization distinct way of life that is common to a particular group of people

civil servant person whose job it is to help run a country or a city

colony settlement in one place by people from another place

contracted allocated to specialist workers in return for pay

deity god or goddess

democracy method of government by which citizens can elect their own rulers

dialogue conversation between two or more people

divulge speak openly about

drachma silver coin that was the main Greek unit of money, worth six *obols*

erosion wearing away over time

frieze carved horizontal band of sculpture that runs around a building

hemlock poisonous plant

hysteria uncontrolled, highly emotional state

idiosyncracy personal peculiarity

indictment (pronounced in-dite-ment) official accusation or charge relating to a crime

inscription writing carved into a surface, such as a monument or a coin

livelihood means of living, income

lyre small, harplike instrument

magistrate officer in charge of enforcement of the law

medlar fruit that resembles a small, brown apple

metic foreigner, with some citizens' rights, living in a Greek city

meticulous very careful

mortar mixture of lime or cement, sand, and water for joining stones or bricks together

mystic spiritual thinker

obol small Greek silver coin. There were six *obols* to a *drachma.*

oracle at Delphi holy place where people consulted their gods for advice or prophecies

overseer supervisor, manager

palaestra open area for practicing combat sports

pediment triangular part that crowns the front of a Greek building

Peloponnese southern region of mainland Greece. This region includes the city-state of Sparta

Persian person who lived in the ancient Middle Eastern kingdom of Persia, which is now known as Iran

philosopher person interested in thoughts and theories, from the Greek words meaning lover of knowledge

polis (more than one are called *poleis*) Greek city-state

precept teaching, words of wisdom

puree paste or soup made from finely ground foods, particularly vegetables

quorum number of people who must be present for the decisions of any assembly to be made official

rustic country dweller

shrine holy place

smelt remove from ore by melting

status position in society

subdivision specialized part or department

taboo forbidden thing

talent very large unit of Greek money (6 *obols* = 1 *drachma*; 100 *drachmas* = 1 *mina*; 60 *minas* = 1 *talent*)

terra-cotta unglazed fine pottery, usually brownish red in color

upper part of a shoe that is not the sole

utopia place where ideal social conditions and government exist

Index